W9-CKM-674

THE AMERICAN REVOLUTION
12 THINGS TO KNOW

by Peggy Caravantes

12 STORY LIBRARY

www.12StoryLibrary.com

12-Story Library is an imprint of Peterson Publishing Company and Press Room Editions.

Produced for 12-Story Library by Red Line Editorial

Photographs ©: Library of Congress, cover, 1, 5, 13, 19, 24; Hemera/Thinkstock, 4; Geo-grafika/iStockphoto, 6; Sarony & Major/Library of Congress, 7; Davidt8, 8; AS400 DB/Corbis, 9; jorgeantonio/iStockphoto/Thinkstock, 11; Cornelius Tiebout/Library of Congress, 12; shakzu/iStockphoto/Thinkstock, 14; Percy Moran/Library of Congress, 15, 20, 28, 29; Photos.com/Thinkstock, 16; John C. McRae/Library of Congress, 21; Public Domain, 22; Godefroy, François/Library of Congress, 23; Fuse/Thinkstock, 25; tupungato/iStockphoto/Thinkstock, 26; alancrosthwaite/iStockphoto/Thinkstock, 27

Content Consultant: Guy Chet, PhD, Professor of Early-American History, Department of History, University of North Texas

Library of Congress Cataloging-in-Publication Data
Names: Caravantes, Peggy, 1935- author.
Title: The American Revolution : 12 things to know / by Peggy Caravantes.
Description: North Mankato, MN : Peterson Publishing Company, 2017. | Series: America at war | Includes bibliographical references and index.
Identifiers: LCCN 2016002052 (print) | LCCN 2016003083 (ebook) | ISBN 9781632352644 (library bound : alk. paper) | ISBN 9781632353146 (pbk. : alk. paper) | ISBN 9781621434337 (hosted ebook)
Subjects: LCSH: United States--History--Revolution, 1775-1783--Juvenile literature.
Classification: LCC E208 .C283 2016 (print) | LCC E208 (ebook) | DDC 973.3--dc23
LC record available at http://lccn.loc.gov/2016002052

Printed in the United States of America
Mankato, MN
May, 2016

Access free, up-to-date content on this topic plus a full digital version of this book. Scan the QR code on page 31 or use your school's login at 12StoryLibrary.com.

Table of Contents

British Place Unfair Taxes on Colonists 4

Colonists Protest with Boston Tea Party 6

Congress Appeals to King George III 8

Paul Revere Warns of British Approach 10

First Shot of American Revolution Fired 12

British Win Battle of Bunker Hill 14

Congress Approves Declaration of Independence 16

George Washington Heads the Continental Army 18

Continental Army Spends Winter at Valley Forge 20

British Surrender at Yorktown 22

Treaty of Paris Brings End to War 24

Colonies Unite under the US Constitution 26

12 Key Dates 28

Glossary 30

For More Information 31

Index 32

About the Author 32

British Place Unfair Taxes on Colonists

Since the early 1600s, Great Britain had ruled the several colonies along the east coast of North America. France controlled large parts of North America known as New France. This area spanned from Louisiana through the Mississippi Valley and the Great Lakes to Canada. During the French and Indian War (1754–1763), the British and the French fought to expand their territory in North America.

After the French and Indian War ended, the British needed money to support their army. They decided to tax American colonists to raise funds. One of the first taxes was the Stamp Act. It was passed on March 22, 1765. It taxed all printed matter. This included newspapers, pamphlets, marriage licenses, playing cards, and wills. British agents stamped the items to prove the tax was paid.

Many colonists opposed the Stamp Act. They complained about the British taxing them without their consent. The colonies had no direct representation in the British government. In protest, many Americans called for a boycott on British goods. A group called

This map shows the 13 original American colonies.

the Sons of Liberty kept British agents from applying the tax. They attacked them and destroyed their stamps and records. They also attacked anyone who did not observe the boycott. Finally, the British government repealed the act.

Tea was a popular drink in the colonies. Perhaps the tax most hated by American colonists was the tax on tea. Great Britain passed the Tea Act in 1773. The East India

13

Number of American colonies.

- The British taxed American colonists to raise money to pay for the French and Indian War.
- The Stamp Act taxed all printed matter.
- The Sons of Liberty tried to stop stamp agents.
- Great Britain passed the Tea Act.
- The British gave the East India Company a monopoly on tea sales.

Company was a major British tea seller. But it had money problems. Through the Tea Act, Great Britain said the East India Company no longer had to pay taxes on tea headed to the American colonies. But other tea importers still had to pay a tax on tea. The act gave the East India Company a monopoly on tea sales. Tea prices dropped, but colonists were unhappy. They were tired of the British government making decisions for them. Colonists wanted to have a voice in the government. Approximately 1,000 people gathered at a meeting in Boston to protest.

Colonists Protest with Boston Tea Party

In 1773, the East India Company loaded its ships with tea and set out for the colonies. When the ships arrived in the colonies, the tea was to be sold by local merchants. But the Sons of Liberty decided to protest. They wanted to keep merchants from buying the tea. They tried to prevent the ships from docking or being unloaded. The ships bound for Philadelphia and New York turned back to Great Britain. Three other ships, the *Beaver*, the *Dartmouth*, and the *Eleanor*, arrived in Boston and docked in the harbor.

British law said cargo on the ships had to be unloaded within 20 days of their arrival. Colonists refused to let them unload. The 20-day waiting period was up on December 16. That night, the Sons of Liberty decided to protest. The men wrapped themselves in blankets. They dressed in costumes, trying to look like Mohawk Indians. They slipped aboard the ships as thousands of people watched from

Colonists were upset about the tea tax because they went through about 1.2 million pounds (544,310 kg) of tea each year.

the shore. The men used axes to smash open 342 tea chests. Then, they dumped the tea into the ocean.

The tea dumped in the ocean during the Boston Tea Party was worth approximately $1.7 million in today's money.

DUMPING THE TEA

Dumping the tea into Boston Harbor was a hard job. A tea chest weighed approximately 400 pounds (181 kg). Sometimes, tea chests were stored under other cargo. This cargo had to be moved to get to the tea. Each chest had to be hauled up on deck. Then, the men had to remove a canvas cover before they could split the chest open with an axe. All the tea in the water caused a terrible smell.

THINK ABOUT IT

Were the Sons of Liberty right to dump the tea into Boston Harbor? Why, or why not? Was there another way they could have protested the taxes?

92,586
Weight, in pounds (41,996 kg), of tea dumped into Boston Harbor.

- Colonists protested the tea tax.
- The Sons of Liberty sneaked onto three British ships loaded with tea.
- They dumped 342 chests of tea into Boston Harbor.
- The harbor was shut down until the colonists paid for the tea.

Congress Appeals to King George III

The British Parliament wanted to punish the Massachusetts colonists for dumping tea into Boston Harbor. They passed the Coercive Acts, known as the Intolerable Acts by the colonists. The Boston Port Act closed the Boston harbor until the town paid for the dumped tea. The Massachusetts Government Act said Great Britain had to approve town meetings. It also said the British government would appoint officials rather than letting the colonists

Carpenter's Hall in Philadelphia was the site of the First Continental Congress.

56
Number of delegates sent to the First Continental Congress.

- The British punished colonists with the Intolerable Acts.
- Delegates from 12 colonies met in Philadelphia for the First Continental Congress on September 5, 1774.
- Delegates adopted the Articles of Association on October 20.
- Congress sent a letter to King George III stating their demands.

Delegates from the North and delegates from the South disagreed about trading goods with the British. The North wanted to stop selling goods to Great Britain. The South said trade was the basis of their economy.

men to represent them. Georgia was preparing for a possible battle with American Indians. It needed British support to pay for the battle and thought taking part in the meeting would anger Great Britain.

The men at the First Continental Congress had never worked together before. At first, they had trouble trusting one another. On October 20, the delegates adopted the Articles of Association. The articles said the colonies would boycott British goods if the Intolerable Acts were not cancelled by December 1, 1774. The articles also said exports to Great Britain would stop if the Intolerable Acts were not lifted by September 10, 1775. Congress then sent a letter to King George III. It said the colonies wanted the Intolerable Acts repealed. They also wanted self-government.

elect them. The Administration of Justice Act said British officials charged with crimes could be tried in Great Britain instead of facing a Massachusetts jury. Colonists called to take part in trials overseas were not paid for time off work and other losses. A fourth act, called the Quartering Act, applied to all of the colonies. It forced them to provide housing, food, and other items to soldiers in their area.

The colonists felt the British acts had taken away their rights. So they united to protest the acts. The First Continental Congress met in Philadelphia on September 5, 1774. Every colony except Georgia sent

Paul Revere Warns of British Approach

The First Continental Congress waited for a response from King George III. In the meantime, colonists began to think about what self-government would look like. When King George III did not reply, the colonists prepared for a possible war with Great Britain. More and more colonists wanted to rebel against British control.

Several towns began to stockpile weapons. An informant told the British governor about the stockpiles in Concord, Massachusetts. British troops were already nearby, in Boston. They were sent to destroy the weapons in Concord.

Colonists learned about the British army's plans and arranged a warning system. They used lanterns as signal lights in the Old North Church in Boston. They made up a code. They would hang one lantern if the British came on land and two if they came by water.

Paul Revere and William Dawes waited for the signal on April 18, 1775. Both men belonged to the Sons of Liberty. They often carried messages between members of the group. When Revere and Dawes saw the flash of two lanterns,

SENDING THE SIGNAL

On the evening of April 18, 1775, two men entered the front door of the Old North Church and locked it. They climbed one of the two staircases in the back corners. Then, they squeezed behind the pipe organ and through a small door to the tower. They had to climb eight flights of stairs in darkness to get to the top. When they reached the top, they leaned out a window to signal with the lanterns.

they set out on horseback to alert villagers in Lexington and Concord. Colonist rebel leaders Samuel Adams and John Hancock were hiding in Lexington. Revere and Dawes wanted to warn them of the British approach.

Dawes traveled on land to Lexington. Revere took a boat across the Charles River to get there. When they left Lexington, the two men started for Concord. But Revere was picked up by a British patrol. They released him after a short time. Still, he did not make it to Concord. Dawes also failed to complete the ride when his horse threw him off. Samuel Prescott, a doctor, had been visiting his girlfriend in Lexington. On the way back to his hometown, he met Revere and Dawes. They told him about what they were doing. He escaped the British patrols that picked up Revere and carried the news to Concord.

Legend says Paul Revere shouted, "The British are coming!" But it is not likely, as it would have drawn British attention.

700
Number of British soldiers who came to Lexington.

- Colonists stockpiled weapons in Concord, Massachusetts.
- The British planned to destroy the weapons.
- Colonists used lanterns to signal British arrival.
- Paul Revere and William Dawes watched for the signal on April 18, 1775.
- Samuel Prescott carried the message to Concord when Revere and Dawes could not.

First Shot of American Revolution Fired

The Lexington colonists knew the British were coming. Some of the town's militia waited for the British to arrive. They called themselves Minutemen. They could be ready to fight at a minute's notice. Their captain told them, "Stand your ground. Don't fire unless fired upon. But if they want to have a war let it begin here."

When the British arrived in Lexington, the Minutemen tried to stop them. Suddenly, a shot rang out. No one was sure who fired it. But it caused others to start shooting. Eight colonists were killed. Ten more were wounded. Only one British soldier was wounded.

After that, the British soldiers moved toward Concord. On the way, they met colonial troops at the North Bridge. There were 500 Minutemen. The British troops numbered approximately 700. But when the Minutemen started firing, the British retreated. The Minutemen hid behind walls, houses, and trees and kept firing at the Redcoats, or British soldiers, as they left Concord.

The Minutemen tried to stop the British at Lexington.

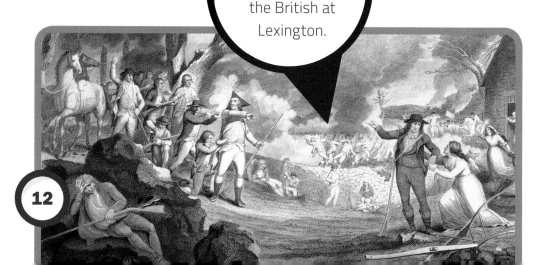

This was not a major battle, but "the shot heard around the world" sent a message to the British army and other colonists. The colonists had proved they could stand up to the British. The American Revolution had begun.

The battleground at Concord

REDCOATS

The British army was known as the Redcoats. They got their name from their red coats. They wore red because the dye was cheapest. They spent hours each day keeping their uniforms spotless. The brass buttons on their coats and their black boots were to be highly polished at all times. On the battlefield, they could tell their own soldiers from their enemies by the color of their coats.

70
Number of Minutemen who met British troops in Lexington.

- Minutemen were waiting for the British when they arrived in Lexington.
- The militia's captain ordered his soldiers not to fire until fired upon.
- A single shot became the initial spark for the American Revolution.
- The two sides met again in Concord, where the British retreated.

British Win Battle of Bunker Hill

After the battles at Lexington and Concord, the British planned to take control of the hills overlooking Boston. They had approximately 10,000 men ready for combat. Their leader was General Thomas Gage.

On June 16, 1775, 1,200 of the Massachusetts militia prepared for the British attack. They were led by Colonel William Prescott. Their plan was to defend Bunker Hill in Charlestown. Instead, for reasons never made clear, Prescott disobeyed orders. He led his men to nearby Breed's Hill instead. Overnight, they built a 6-foot (1.8-m) earthen wall to protect themselves from British gunfire.

The next morning, three British warships fired on the colonists. Most of the shells went into the side of Breed's Hill. The British could not angle their guns high enough for their shots to

A statue of Colonel William Prescott can be found near the Bunker Hill Memorial in Charlestown, Massachusetts.

COLONEL
WILLIAM PRESCOTT

The Battle of Bunker Hill is misnamed. It was actually fought on Breed's Hill.

reach the earthen wall at the top of the hill. They decided to attack from a different direction. Twenty-eight barges carried 1,500 Redcoats to the other side of the hill.

The colonists held their ground until they ran out of ammunition. Great Britain won the battle and took over the hill. But the British suffered many deaths, and many men were wounded. The British commander in chief, William Howe, said, "The success is too dearly bought."

226
Number of British soldiers killed on Breed's Hill.

- Great Britain wanted control of Boston.
- Colonel William Prescott led colonists to Breed's Hill instead of Bunker Hill.
- Colonial troops built an earthen fort for protection.
- The battle moved to hand-to-hand combat.
- Great Britain won the battle but at a heavy loss of life.

Congress Approves Declaration of Independence

In 1775, 65 delegates attended the Second Continental Congress. They met in the Pennsylvania State House in Philadelphia on May 10. It was the first time all 13 colonies were represented.

The delegates talked about King George III's failure to respond to their demands. At first, they could not agree about how they should react. Some wanted to try again to get the king to restore their rights. But others disagreed. The British had used force against them at the Battle of Lexington and the Battle of Concord. In the end, the colonists decided to fight back. The delegates then planned to raise funds to form the

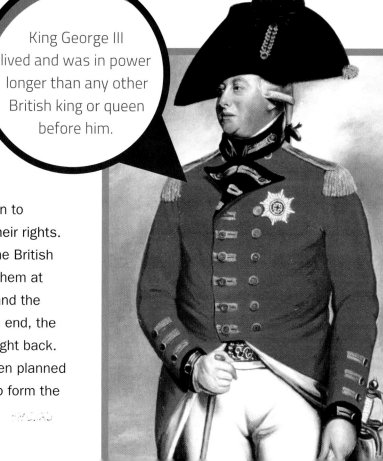

King George III lived and was in power longer than any other British king or queen before him.

Continental Army. Each state had to provide men for one year's service.

The colonies talked about why they felt independence from Great Britain was necessary. They said

500

Number of copies of the Declaration of Independence immediately printed and distributed throughout the newly formed United States of America.

- Delegates from all of the 13 colonies met at the Second Continental Congress.
- They established a Continental Army.
- They wrote the Declaration of Independence, separating the colonies from Great Britain.
- July 4, 1776, became the nation's birthday.

THE LIBERTY BELL

The Liberty Bell was constructed in 1751. It cracked during a test but was recast. The most famous ringing of the bell was on July 8, 1776. It called the people of Philadelphia together to hear a reading of the Declaration of Independence. The recast bell broke in 1835. In 1846, the crack grew in size when the bell was rung to celebrate George Washington's birthday. It could not be fixed.

the British government had broken laws. It had made choices based on whims rather than laws. And it had denied colonists the right to self-government. Then, the colonies began working on the Declaration of Independence. This document stated the colonies were no longer under British rule. They were now a new country called the United States of America. The declaration also said all men are created equal. They have certain rights, including "life, liberty, and the pursuit of happiness."

In July 1775, the Congress reached out to the British again to ask for their rights to be restored. When the British did not respond, the Congress decided to move ahead with the Declaration of Independence. Over the winter of 1775 to 1776, the Congress worked on the document. It was adopted on July 4, 1776. This date became the new nation's birthday.

8

George Washington Heads the Continental Army

Delegates at the Second Continental Congress chose George Washington to lead the Continental Army. He had some battle experience in the French and Indian War. But he had been retired from military duty for 15 years. Still, he agreed to serve as commander in chief.

Washington faced a huge challenge. His soldiers were ordinary men with little or no battle experience. And his small army was outnumbered by British troops.

Washington's Continental Army endured several defeats throughout 1775 and 1776. He knew he needed to do something different. Washington went on the offensive. On Christmas night in 1776, he led his small remaining army of 2,400 men across the ice-filled Delaware River. At Trenton, New Jersey, they made a surprise attack on Hessian mercenaries hired by the British. The cold winds

HESSIANS

The Hessians were German soldiers hired by the British during the American Revolution. Their name came from Hesse-Cassel, the home state of most of the troops. The Hessian government earned money by renting soldiers to the British.

and deep snow had muffled the Americans' approach. The Hessians were still inside their quarters when Washington's army attacked. More than 1,000 Hessians were captured.

Washington's win at Trenton was followed by a few more small wins. Each victory improved the soldiers' spirits and inspired more men to join the army. On October 7, 1777, the US and British troops fought in the Battle of Saratoga. The British gave up when they were surrounded by

13,000 to 17,000 US troops. The victory had a great effect on future US successes.

In 1778, France joined the Americans in their fight against Great Britain. The British and French were longtime enemies. With the US victories of 1777, France saw a chance to gain an ally. It provided money, supplies, weapons, and more soldiers to aid the US army.

Washington crossing the Delaware River to battle the Hessians

43

Washington's age when he became commander in chief of the Continental Army.

- On December 25, 1776, Washington led his army in an attack on the Hessians.
- Victory at the Battle of Saratoga on October 7, 1777, was a turning point in the war.
- In 1778, France began to support the US army.

THINK ABOUT IT

France helped the United States during its war against Great Britain. Do you think the United States would still have won the war without France's help? Why, or why not?

9

Continental Army Spends Winter at Valley Forge

The winter of 1777 to 1778 brought new problems for the Continental Army. Washington and his men retreated to Valley Forge. Only 8,000 of his men were still fit for duty. Most had only the ragged clothing they wore. There were no coats or blankets. Many were barefoot.

Washington chose the area because it provided natural protection. A river was on one side, with a creek on the other. Tree-covered hills allowed the army to watch for any British soldiers who might approach. But there were no buildings to shelter the men from the cold weather.

Washington had his men build log cabins. Each hut was 14 by 16 feet (4.3 by 4.9 m) and held

George Washington and his troops were starving when they arrived at Valley Forge.

12 men. The men slept on the floors. Cold air leaked into the poorly built cabins. Lack of food was also a problem. The men had no meat or vegetables. They lived on nothing but firecake for two months. Diseases spread throughout the camp.

A Prussian military officer, Baron von Steuben, came to the men's aid. He had been recommended by the French to bring organization and discipline to the US troops. France feared the money it sent the Americans to support the war was not being well spent. By spring, the US troops were more organized and better trained. They left Valley Forge ready to continue fighting.

George Washington prayed for his men and his country at Valley Forge.

2,000
Number of men who died during the long winter at Valley Forge.

- Washington's army settled at Valley Forge for the 1777 to 1778 winter.
- There was no housing, and clothing, shoes, and food were scarce.
- A Prussian officer, Baron von Steuben, helped to train the army.

THINK ABOUT IT

Pretend you are a soldier spending the winter at Valley Forge. Write a letter to your family describing the experience.

10

British Surrender at Yorktown

By 1778, the British were focused on a war with France. They were upset France had allied with the United States. The British had fewer soldiers to fight in the United States. They offered to end the war by agreeing to many of the terms set out by the First and Second Continental Congress. But the Americans refused. They would only settle if Great Britain recognized US independence and removed its troops from the new republic. The war was not over.

In late 1778, British General Charles Cornwallis decided to take his army to the southern states. With little success in the North, Cornwallis thought his army might do better in the South. There, he hoped to cut off supplies and soldiers going to Washington's army. By May 1780, Cornwallis and the British occupied Savannah, Georgia, and Charleston, South Carolina.

Later that year, Washington sent one of his best generals, Nathanael Greene, to the South. There, Greene would lead US troops against Cornwallis. The two sides clashed in the Carolinas. They fought at such battles as King's Mountain, Cowpens, and

Nathanael Greene became quartermaster general of the Continental Army on March 2, 1778.

Guilford Courthouse. Great Britain suffered heavy losses of soldiers.

Cornwallis moved his troops to Virginia in 1781. There, he planned to wait for more supplies and troops from Great Britain. In August, he camped near the village of Yorktown, Virginia. By that time, 7,000 French soldiers had joined Washington's army near New York City. The combined US and French forces set out on the 200-mile (322-km) march to Yorktown.

Meanwhile, 36 French warships kept the British navy from removing Cornwallis's army or supporting it by sending more supplies and soldiers. By October 1781, Washington's 20,000 soldiers had surrounded 9,500 British troops. Cornwallis requested a ceasefire on October 17, 1781. His troops had suffered many losses, and they had no way to escape. Cornwallis sent his deputy to offer his sword in surrender, claiming he was sick. The signing of the surrender papers took place on October 19, 1781.

Cornwallis surrendered at Yorktown, Virginia.

15

Number of days it took Washington's army to march from New York to Yorktown.

- Both armies moved to the South because of a long standstill in the North.
- The French aided US troops with supplies and men.
- By October 1781, Washington's troops had surrounded the British at Yorktown.
- General Cornwallis surrendered to Washington on October 17, 1781.
- The surrender papers were signed on October 19, 1781.

Treaty of Paris Brings End to War

Talks to bring a formal end to the war started in April 1782. The United States and Great Britain finally signed the Treaty of Paris on September 3, 1783. It brought an official end to the American Revolution. The treaty proclaimed the United States' independence from Great Britain. It also provided expanded boundaries for the new nation. The Mississippi River became the western border. The Great Lakes were the new northern border. US fishermen were guaranteed fishing rights off the coast of Newfoundland.

Throughout the war, some Americans remained loyal to Great Britain. They were known as Loyalists. The United States agreed to try to stop state and local governments from mistreating Loyalists. As well, governments were ordered to return property taken from Loyalists during the war.

Benjamin Franklin, John Adams, and John Jay were chosen by

In spring 1782, Great Britain sent Scottish merchant Richard Oswald to Paris to meet with Benjamin Franklin. The two men talked about peace terms.

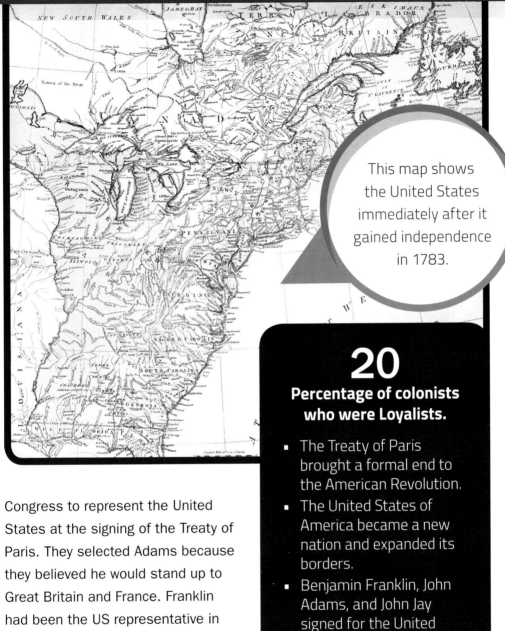

This map shows the United States immediately after it gained independence in 1783.

20
Percentage of colonists who were Loyalists.

- The Treaty of Paris brought a formal end to the American Revolution.
- The United States of America became a new nation and expanded its borders.
- Benjamin Franklin, John Adams, and John Jay signed for the United States.
- David Hartley, a member of British Parliament, signed on behalf of King George III.
- Both countries finally approved the agreement in 1784.

Congress to represent the United States at the signing of the Treaty of Paris. They selected Adams because they believed he would stand up to Great Britain and France. Franklin had been the US representative in France since 1776. Jay was a lawyer already working in Europe to form other alliances. A member of British Parliament, David Hartley, signed for King George III. Both countries finally approved the agreement in 1784. They then exchanged signed copies.

Colonies Unite under the US Constitution

During the war, a constitution was written. It created a weak central government. And the states were self-governing. A few years after the war, some Americans sought a new constitution. They wanted to create a stronger central government. They also wanted to limit the sovereignty of each state.

All states except Rhode Island sent delegates to Philadelphia for a constitutional convention. They met in the summer of 1787, from May 25 to September 17. The purpose of the meeting was to create the US Constitution. This document would explain how the national, or federal, government would operate. All states would be required to follow the Constitution.

Large and small states disagreed about how each would be represented in the new national government. The larger states wanted the number of delegates to be based on the state's population. The smaller states objected. They finally agreed on a two-house legislature. In the lower house, or House of Representatives, each state would be represented

Together, the House of Representatives and the Senate are known as Congress. Congress meets at the Capitol Building in Washington, DC.

8

Number of years the American Revolution lasted.

- Delegates from all states except Rhode Island met in 1787 to organize the US government.
- They chose a two-house legislature that included the House of Representatives and the Senate.
- They discussed who should have voting rights and how to elect a president.
- The Constitution was ratified in 1788.
- Washington was elected president and John Adams vice president.

Over the years, there have been 27 amendments to the US Constitution.

In 1789, the new government was formed. George Washington was elected as US president, with John Adams as his vice president. Then, they started work on the Bill of Rights. It is made up of the first 10 amendments to the Constitution. These amendments restricted the power of the new federal government.

according to population. The greater the population of the state, the more representatives it would have. In the upper house, or Senate, each state would have two delegates.

Next, the men debated voting rights and how to elect a president. The Constitution had to be ratified by at least nine states before it went into effect. By the end of 1788, 11 states had ratified it.

After years of fighting for independence, the colonies were officially free of British rule. The United States was now an independent nation with its own system of government.

12 Key Dates

March 22, 1765
Great Britain passes the Stamp Act, the first of many taxes on the colonies.

December 16, 1773
The Sons of Liberty dump tea in Boston Harbor.

September 5, 1774
The First Continental Congress meets.

April 19, 1775
The Battles of Lexington and Concord start the American Revolution.

May 10, 1775
The Second Continental Congress meets.

June 16, 1775
Colonial and British troops clash at Breed's Hill.

July 4, 1776
Delegates sign the Declaration of Independence.

December 25, 1776
George Washington leads troops across the frozen Delaware River. They capture 1,000 Hessians.

October 7, 1777
US troops defeat the British at the Battle of Saratoga.

October 17, 1781
British General Cornwallis surrenders at the Battle of Yorktown.

September 3, 1783
The signing of the Treaty of Paris brings a formal end to the American Revolution.

May 25, 1787
The Constitutional Convention begins in Philadelphia.

Glossary

adopted
Put into action.

amendment
A change to a law or legal document.

artillery
Large, powerful guns.

delegate
A person who represents others.

firecake
Bread made from a mixture of flour and water cooked over an open flame.

intolerable
Impossible to endure.

mercenaries
Soldiers hired to serve in a foreign army.

militia
A group of people who are trained to fight but are not professional soldiers.

monopoly
The complete possession or control of the supply of a product or service.

ratify
To give official approval.

repealed
Formally annulled or withdrawn.

republic
A state in which the people and their elected leaders have supreme power, as well as an elected president.

standstill
A complete halt.

stockpile
To gather a large supply of food or weapons to keep from running out or facing an emergency in the future.

30

For More Information

Books

Murray, Stuart. *DK Eyewitness Books: American Revolution*. New York: DK Children, 2015.

Schanzer, Rosalyn. *George vs. George: The American Revolution as Seen from Both Sides*. Washington, DC: National Geographic Children's Books, 2007.

Sheinkin, Steve. *King George: What Was His Problem? The Whole Hilarious Story of the American Revolution*. New York: Square Fish, 2009.

Visit 12StoryLibrary.com

Scan the code or use your school's login at **12StoryLibrary.com** for recent updates about this topic and a full digital version of this book. Enjoy free access to:

- Digital ebook
- Breaking news updates
- Live content feeds
- Videos, interactive maps, and graphics
- Additional web resources

Note to educators: Visit 12StoryLibrary.com/register to sign up for free premium website access. Enjoy live content plus a full digital version of every 12-Story Library book you own for every student at your school.

Index

Adams, John, 24–25, 27

Baron von Steuben, 21
Battle of Bunker Hill, 14–15
Bill of Rights, 27
Boston, 5, 6–7, 8, 10, 14–15
Breed's Hill, 14–15

Coercive Acts, 8–9
colonies, 4–5, 6, 8–9, 16–17, 26–27
Concord, 10–11, 12–13, 14, 16
Continental Army, 16–17, 18–19, 20–21, 22
Cornwallis, Charles, 22–23

Dawes, William, 10–11
Declaration of Independence, 16–17

East India Company, 5, 6
First Continental Congress, 8–9, 10, 22
France, 4, 19, 21, 22, 25
Franklin, Benjamin, 24–25

Gage, Thomas, 14
Great Britain, 4–5, 6, 8–9, 10, 15, 16–17, 19, 22–23, 24–25
Great Lakes, 4, 24
Greene, Nathanael, 22

Jay, John, 24–25

King George III, 8, 9–10, 16

Lexington, 11, 12–13, 14, 16

Prescott, William, 14–15

Revere, Paul, 10–11

Second Continental Congress, 16–17, 18, 22
Sons of Liberty, 4–5, 6–7, 10
Stamp Act, 4–5

Tea Tax, 5, 6–7
Treaty of Paris, 24–25

Valley Forge, 20–21

Washington, George, 17, 18–19, 20–21, 22–23, 27

Yorktown, 22–23

About the Author

Prize-winning author Peggy Caravantes has written more than 20 children's and young adult nonfiction books. She especially enjoys the research that forms the basis of the books. A former teacher, she lives in San Antonio, Texas.

READ MORE FROM 12-STORY LIBRARY

Every 12-Story Library book is available in many formats. For more information, visit 12StoryLibrary.com.